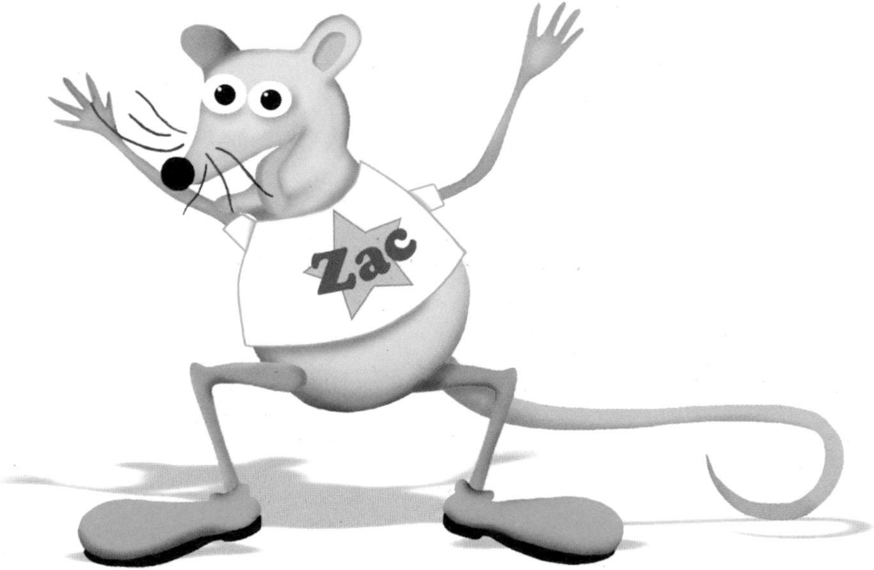

Zac is a rat.

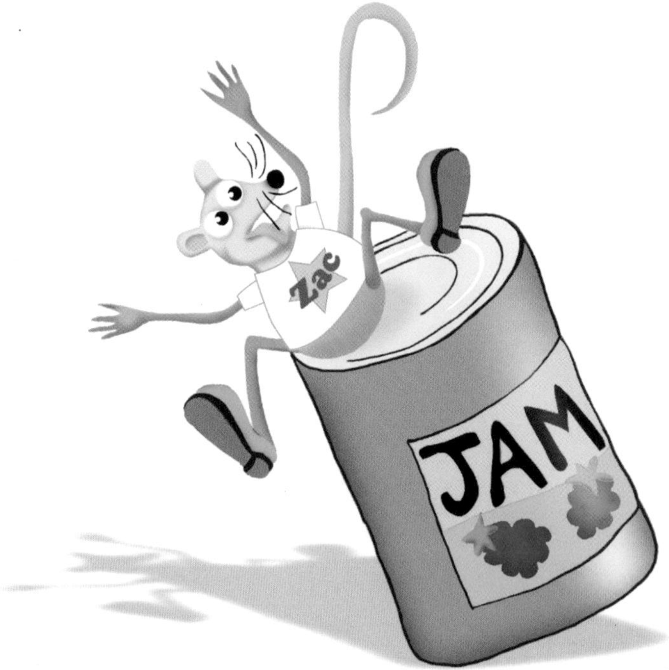

Zac sat on a can.

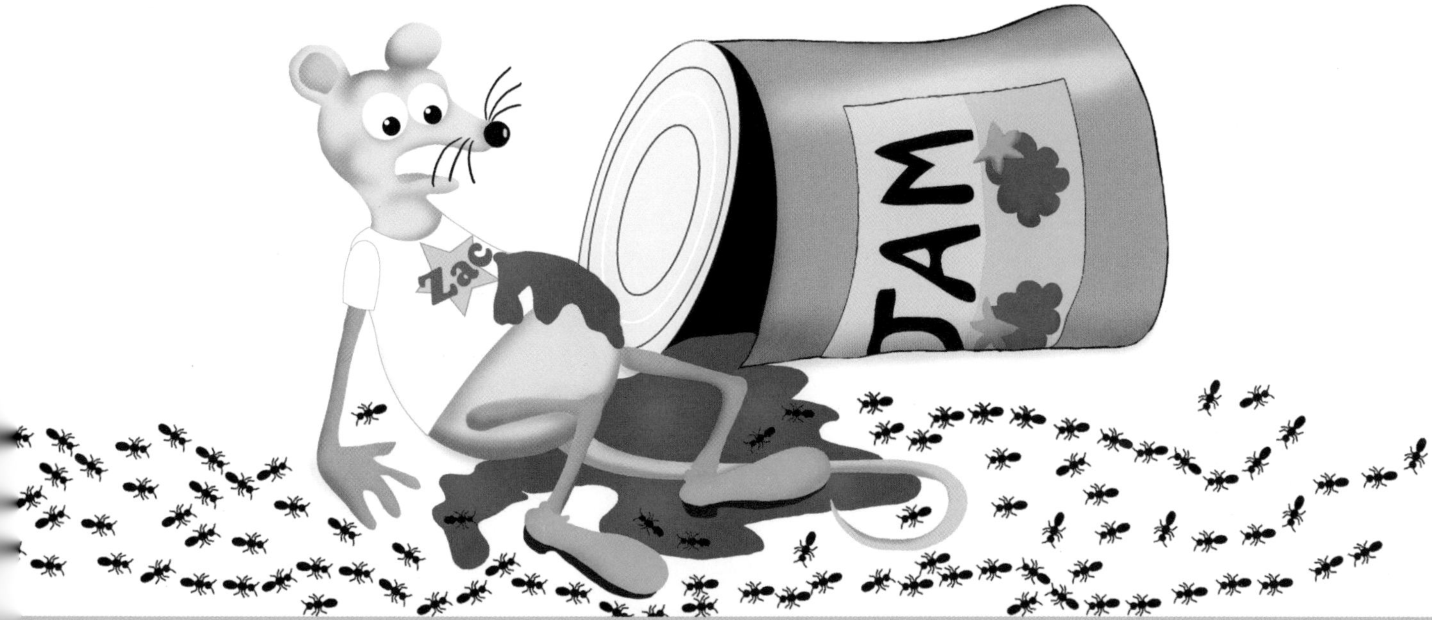

The ants ran to the jam.

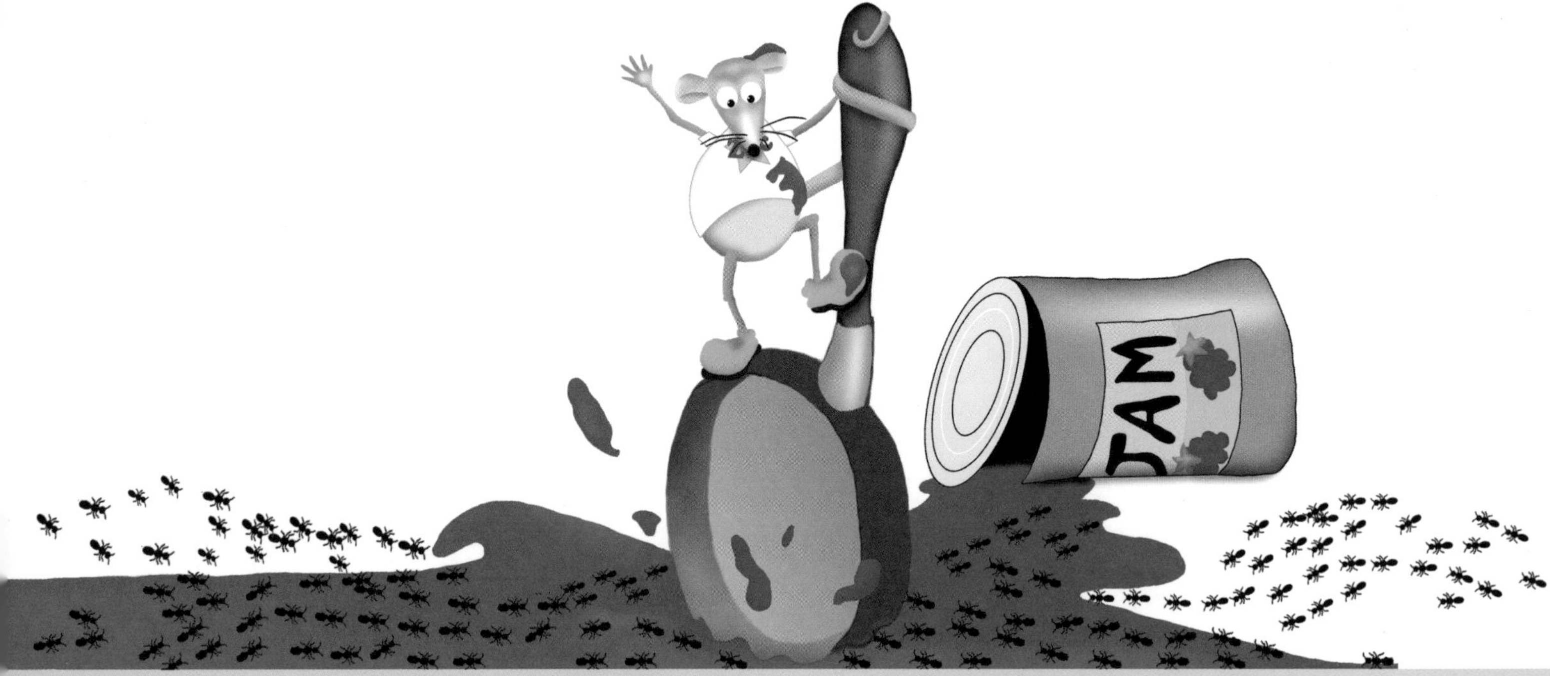

Zac had a pan.

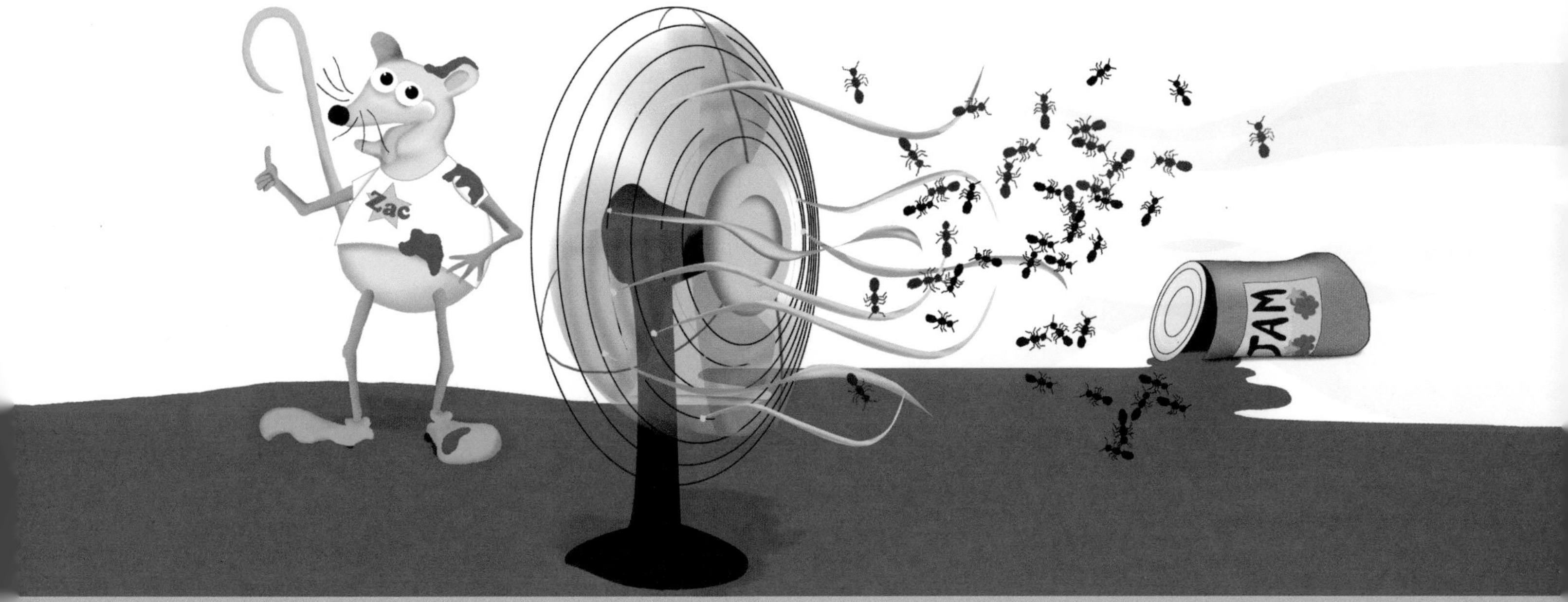

Zac had a fan.

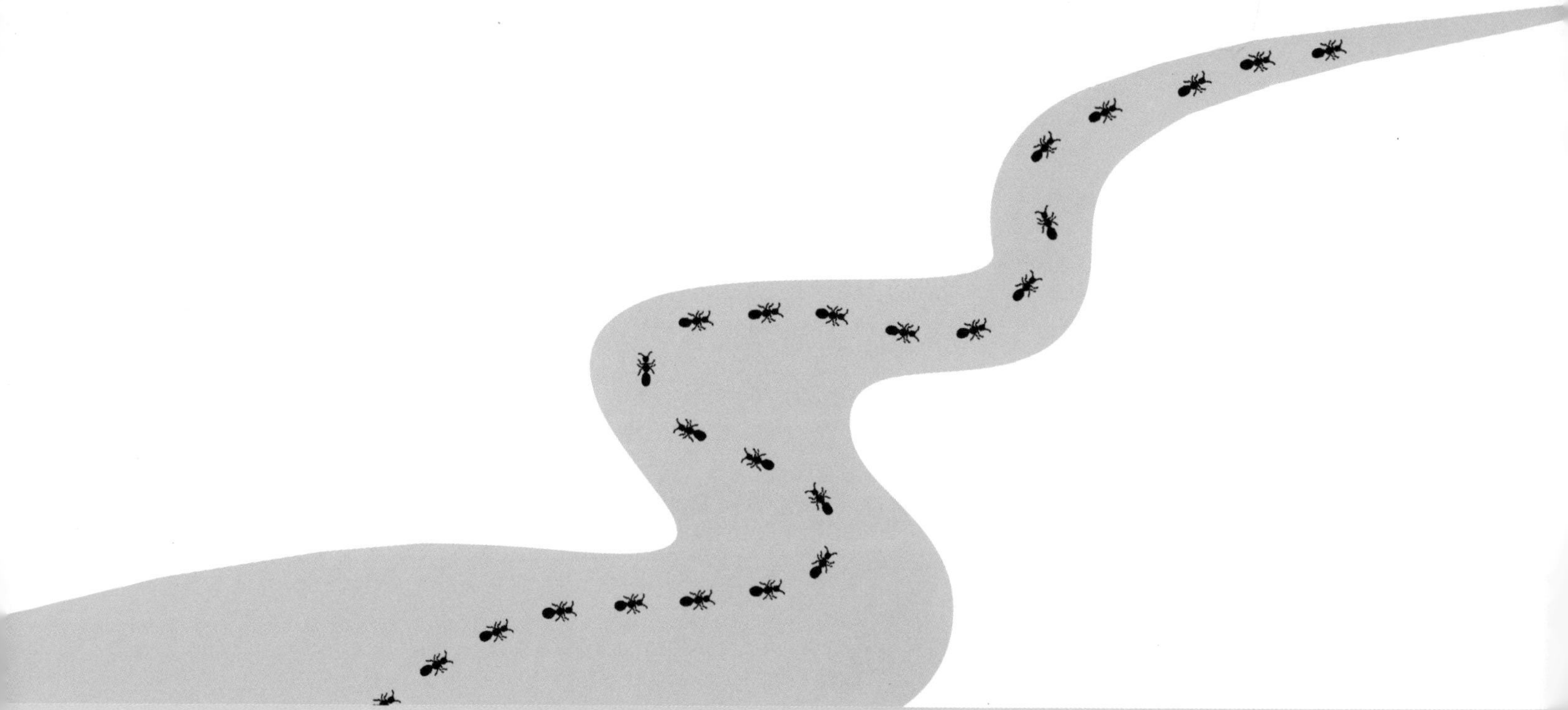

The ants ran and ran.

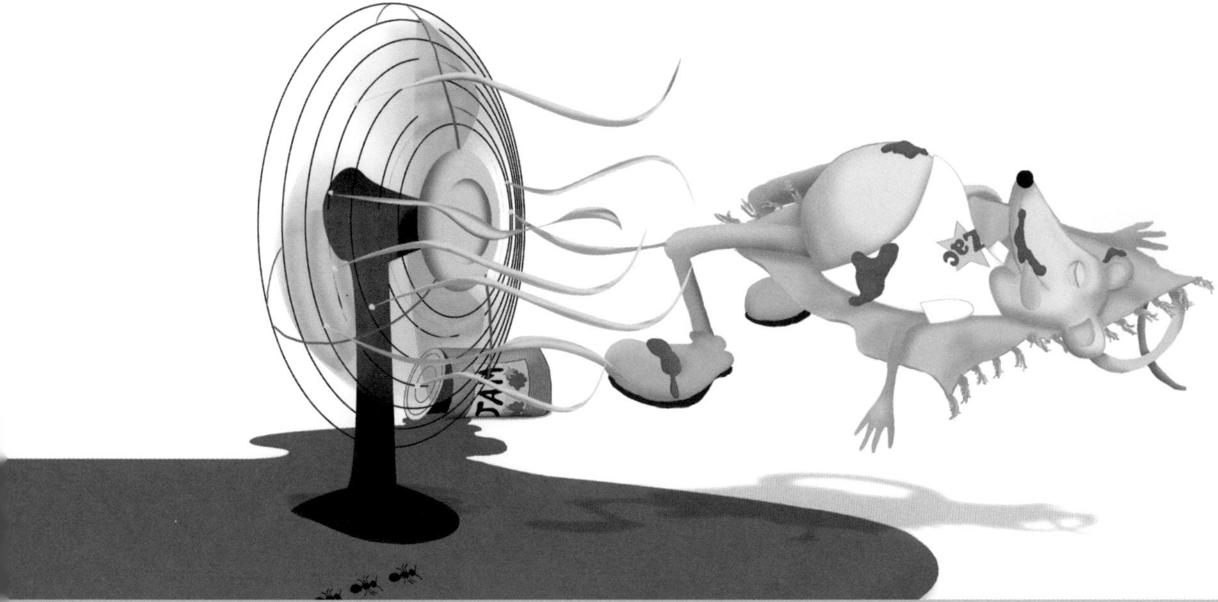

Zac had a nap.

The end